owner of this book & grower of LOVE

Text and illustrations copyright © 2018 by Kimberly Wyman
All rights reserved.

This book, or parts thereof, may not be reproduced in any form without permission in writing from the author. The scanning, uploading, and distribution of this book via the Internet or via any other means without permission of the author is illegal and punishable by law.

Please purchase only authorized electronic editions, and do not participate in or encourage electronic piracy of copyrighted materials. Your support of the author's right is appreciated.

Published by MiKaa Creative, LLC.
Printed and bound in China
ISBN: 978-0-9985282-0-5

Library of Congress Control Number: 2017917170

www.xoKimberlyWyman.com

Grow LOVE

words and pictures by

Kimberly Wyman

To Aeson and Aiya who
effortlessly Grow LOVE every day.

To Troy who taught me that
accepting love is just as important as giving love.

LOVE washes away hurt and heals wounds big and small.

With something as good as this, of course we want more.

Where can we find it?
Can we get it at the store?

You won't find LOVE on a shelf, because it's not something that you buy.

When you give something away, it's gone and forever out of sight.

But not with LOVE...
it's very magical.

Its powers and spells
are quite fantastical.

When you LOVE a person, it doesn't take your LOVE from another.

there's always so much LOVE to find and give.

Today's Menu

Indian Shortbread Cookies

Ingredients

1 1/2 cup flour
1/2 tsp baking soda
1/4 tsp cardamom powder
small pinch of salt
1/2 cup powdered sugar
1/2 cup butter (1 stick) or ghee (room temperature)
1/4 tsp cinnamon
bit of milk (if dry)

Directions

Mix flour, baking soda, cardamom, cinnamon and salt.

Cream butter and sugar.

Combine dry ingredients with butter and sugar mix.

Refrigerate dough for 15 minutes and then make small balls and flatten. If the cookies are too dry, you can brush the cookies with a bit of milk.

Bake at 350 for 10-12 minutes; do not overbake.

Let cookies cool before moving them off tray.

made with LOVE

So give someone a smile or a pat on the back.

So get busy, start doing what you do.

There are so many different ways to say, "I LOVE you."

Let's Grow more LOVE
www.GrowLoveBook.com

Our Arctic Animal Friends

Over at our website, you'll learn more about our arctic animal friends:

Harp Seal	**Arctic Hare**	**Snow Goose**
Snowy Owl	Ermine	Dall Sheep
Arctic Fox	**Polar Bear**	**Orca**
Walrus	Ribbon Seal	Moose
Penguin	**Puffin**	**Narwhal**
Reindeer	Arctic Wolf	

Discover the names of each arctic animal friend, what some of their hobbies are, and how they prefer to Grow LOVE.

Odd One Out

All of the friends in this book are from the arctic,
Except for one, that was added as a trick.

Do you know which animal doesn't live in the Northern Hemisphere?
Is it a moose, ermine, penguin, or maybe the reindeer?

Try your best and take another long look.
Can you find who doesn't belong in this book?

When you're done, see if you're right
by going online and checking the website.

Which seeds will you plant to Grow LOVE?

Baking for other people is such a great way to **Grow LOVE!** Try the recipe in this book for Indian Shortbread (Naan Khatai) adapted from Handstand Kids and contributed by Sharon NDiaye. Sharon teaches multicultural cooking classes for children in Westchester County, NY. Find Sharon on Instagram at @cookingwithkidsNY
Visit our website for more great kid friendly recipes!

- ☐ **Draw a picture for your neighbor**
- ☐ **Sing a song to someone in your family**
- ☐ _____
- ☐ _____
- ☐ _____
- ☐ _____
- ☐ _____

AUTHOR'S NOTE

My journey creating Grow LOVE started a couple years ago. It was born from a desire of raising my children as global citizens. That passion led me down a path of research and exploration. I quickly learned being a global citizen extends beyond observing and respecting varied cultures. It's an ideology of a type of person you wish to embody and the impact you make on the world.

All of that starts with LOVE. By discovering at a young age that we can all Grow LOVE in a lot of different ways, it brings us closer to being one global community with peace and acceptance.

Personally, it affects my family because we are an adoptive, multi-cultural family. As a global family, I must instill the importance of equality and social justice. In my heart, I believe it doesn't matter where you were born or where you reside. Being born on a particular piece of land may make you lucky, but does not deem you more deserving than anyone else. We all should have the same access to the basic necessities of life. We should all be gifted the same opportunities. We're all human and our differences should be embraced and similarities celebrated.

Together, let's Grow LOVE...a whole bunch of LOVE!

Kimberly Wyman loves to string words and pictures together for families built by love, not necessarily biology. She's a creative who writes with the intention of BIGS reading to littles to share moments of love and connection.

As a global mom of a multicultural family, Kimberly's passion is in helping families raise healthy and happy global citizens. She is crazy about her family, adoption, thoughtful designs, open spaces, creating almost anything, and homemade whipped cream.

Kimberly is also the author of "You are my baby. I am your mommy."

www.xoKimberlyWyman.com